Jay Stielstra and Friends Playing on Waters Road, Ann Arbor, 1986

*For Jarrett Dieterlee
From Jay
Oct. 12, 2022 - Leland - the Old Art Building*

Heaven for Me

Selected Lyrics and Scores by
JAY STIELSTRA

with introductions by
*Chris Buhalis, Lana Pollack,
Dick Siegel, and Dave Siglin*

edited by
Nada Rakic and Barbara Schmid

music editor
Judy Banker

All lyrics and scores © Jay Stielstra

ISBN 978-0-578-52628-7
© 2019 Nada Rakic

Cover: South Branch of the Au Sable River, Michigan
   Design by Kay Clahassey
   Photo by Nada Rakic

Table of Contents

Foreword ....*v*
    Nada Rakic

Acknowledgements ....*vii*
    Nada Rakic

Songs Travel with Us through Life...*viii*
    Chris Buhalis

Not Far from Home ....*ix*
    Lana Pollack

I Love Jay's Songs Because ....*xi*
    Dick Siegel

A Diamond in Our Midst ....*xiv*
    Dave Siglin

Biography of Jay Stielstra ....*xv*
    Barbara Schmid

Heaven for Me 1
    Road Less Traveled 2
    Going Home 4
    Cross Over the Line 6
    I'm Singin' 8
    Never Been Much of a Ramblin' Man 12
    Manistee Waltz 14
    Black River Jones 18
    Boats Came in to Ludington 20
    The Lake 22
    Cut River Bridge 26
    Heaven for Me 28

Memories to Hold 31
    Baker's Daughter 32
    November Love 34
    Wednesday's Child 36
    I Love Two Rivers and Only One Woman 40
    So Easy 42

Fragile Thing 44
Times that We Had 46
I'll Remember 48
Don't Let Me Down Easy 50
Last Night You Came Alive Again 52
Far Side of the Bed 54
Darlin' Except You 56
Lord, What Do We Know? 58
Most I'm Missing You 60
A Fool for Lovin' You 62
Read Between the Lines 64
Red Rose 66
Barbara's Waltz 68
It's a Wonder 70

Hands of Time 73
Hands of Time 74
I Come Down from My Home Town 76
Hangin' 'Round the Bars in Town 78
Pitcher and a Glass 80
The Old Brown Bottle 82
Armistice Day Storm 84
Rolling Along 88
No Fool Like an Old Fool 90
Lie of the Mind 92
To Say Goodbye 94
Suino's Song 96
Farewell to One and All 98
Hey Buddy, It's Still Me 100

Destruction's Its Own Penalty 103
Liam O'Reilly 104
Linebacker from Muskegon 106
Leave the Bottle on the Table, Waiter 110
Are You Comin' Are You Goin' 112
Turning the World into Texas 116
Never Been to Dixie 120
Tittabawassee Jane 122
Where Have All the White Pines Gone, Daddy 124
Same Folks We Hated in High School 126

Credits 129

Jay Stielstra Discography 131

Foreword

Perhaps one of the most accurate descriptions of Jay Stielstra is by Sandor Slomovits: "Jay Stielstra is one of the most humble, self-effacing guys you'll ever meet. Which just goes to show that it is possible for ego and talent to co-exist in an inverse ratio. Once you hear a Stielstra song, you quickly realize that despite his aw-shucks demeanor, he's one hell of a song writer." ("Jay Stielstra: Virtuoso songwriter and human," *Ann Arbor Observer*, November 2015).

Short but expressive, picturesque, and so true is also the remark by Chris Buhalis, who, as a fellow musician, often has the role of introducing Jay to an audience – to paraphrase him: if I praise him and pay tribute to Jay's importance and achievements, which he certainly deserves, he'll give me "that look."

It is not an easy task to reconcile the greatness of this bard of the Michigan musical scene with the modesty and humility of his character. Precisely because of that, and the possibility that "that look" will be directed at me, my proposal for this book was not made directly to Jay himself. I used that old wisdom that the easiest way to reach a man is through his better half. This proved to be a good decision for various reasons. Jay's wife, Barbara Schmid, listened to my proposition with great attention, brought it to Jay, and, to my delight, he agreed, and we started our work on the book.

In several discussions with Barbara, who was my essential collaborator, we put together the initial concept for the book. Alongside Jay's lyrics, evocative illustrations and images, we decided to include musical scores. Jay's rich poetical opus comprises around 180 songs. Barbara made a first selection of 90 songs, which I was supposed to reduce to around 40 (according to Jay's suggestion). In the end, we all came to a selection of 52. The decision of which songs to include, and which not, was not easy to make because a great number of Jay's lyrics reach the level of fine poetry and deserve to be perpetuated in printed form. If mistakes have been made in our selection, they are mine.

At the heart of Stielstra's poetry is his personal world, rich, diverse, often reexamined. He writes about the beauty of nature and his Michigan origins, love, the impermanence of things, suffering, and worries, crystalizing his transcendent knowledge and self-knowledge as well as his understanding of the truths of life and the world, society and social phenomena. His artistic expression of these themes is characterized by simplicity, clarity, immediacy, emotional warmth, and above all a sincere approach.

Precisely that diversity of Jay's poetry defined the concept and structure of this book. The songs are divided into four thematic sections: *Heaven for Me* (songs about Michigan), *Times That We Had* (love songs), *Hands of Time* (songs about impermanence and the passing of time), and *Destruction's Its Own Penalty* (environmental, anti-war, political, and social justice songs). All sections are named from titles or the lyrics of Jay's songs. It is easy to see that the first song, *Road Less Traveled*, does not belong thematically to the section *Heaven for Me*, but it seems to me that it dramatically portrays the return of the poet to the place he belongs, his beloved Michigan, as expressed explicitly in the immediately following song, *Going Home*.

Although Jay Stielstra's poetry has all the qualities necessary to stand alone, by itself, this book would be incomplete without musical scores. Jay may appear to be shy, but he is far from shy when it comes to sharing his music with other musicians. I don't believe that I exaggerate if I say that well over several dozen musicians have presented Jay's songs or have them in their repertoire. With both lyrics and musical scores, sharing should be available to both already established musicians and musicians who are just emerging.*

And now on a very personal note: This book is my way of saying thank you to Jay Stielstra.

His musical *North Country Opera* was the first theater show that I saw in this country, and he was one of the first people that I met. Coming from a country (the former Yugoslavia) that I was losing at that time to a bloody and senseless war, thanks to his lyrics I was gaining new one here in Michigan, especially northern Michigan to which I am now frequently "crossing over the line."

During the war, I was working on a radio show for WUOM, "The Spirit of Sarajevo" (Sarajevo is the capital city of Bosnia, part of Yugoslavia, and in that time was under siege), and I wanted to include the famous Bosnian love song *Emina* in the show, but performed by an American. Who else to ask for that than Jay? He learned a few verses (in Bosnian!) and sang it so beautifully that it reduced many of the Bosnians to tears. In that time of ethnic cleansing, this beloved love song, written by a Serb, Aleksa Šantić, about love for a beautiful Muslim girl, Emina, became in a way a cry for unity in Bosnia. I am grateful to Jay for evoking those feelings with his singing.

I'm also thankful to Jay for trusting me to direct his play *A Better Way to Die*, although he knew very well that my English was not adequate for even a simple conversation, let alone complex professional work. In that situation, though, I didn't have a choice. I started expressing ideas and myself in English. This was my starting point for speaking English, however awkwardly.

Now, if I get "that look" that Chris Buhalis was taking about, so be it. I'll take it, because with this book I spoke my mind as honestly as I can.

Nada Rakic

---

* The majority of Jay's songs have never been notated. The many artists who have performed or recorded them have used the lyrics or guitar chords Jay wrote down or provided from memory. As in the true folk tradition, these performers may have changed the lyrics and melodies to suit their style and interpretation of the song. For this book, we've based the notation, chords, and lyrics as closely as possible on the way that Jay performs them.

Judy Banker, Musical Editor

Acknowledgements

Thanks to Dick Coffey for giving me initial directions to the Upper and Lower Manistee River and the CCC Bridge. Along the way I took some pictures, a couple of which are in this book.

Special thanks to Charlie Weaver who guided me along the Manistee River and showed me the big tree with a vertical split in its trunk facing the Mecum Road where it crosses Sunset Trail. This is the so-called "Mecum Bar," referred to in Jay's song *Manistee Waltz*, where Jay and his fellow fishermen stashed their beer to stay cold until they took a break from fishing and came back to drink, talk, tell lies, and have a good time, according to Charlie.

"Will the beer stay cold in the Mecum Bar"
(Manistee Waltz)

It was a great privilege and pleasure to work with Kay Clahassey on the illustrations, images, and cover of this book. When I asked her to help, she accepted without hesitation, calling it a "labor of love." Knowing Jay, and having done graphic art for several programs of his musicals, she immediately grasped the entire concept of this book and its importance and meaning as a tribute to him. Her contributions of ideas, images, and esthetics, along with her excellent artistic thinking and skills improved the book a great deal. Thank you, Kay.

The greatest thanks goes to my husband, Bob Whallon. He unselfishly invested an enormous number of hours, as well as his expertise and technical knowledge in the preparation of books for printing. There are no words that can express the debt I owe to him.

Nada Rakic

Songs Travel with Us through Life

These pages contain songs written by Jay Stielstra.

They are honest songs. Hard working songs. Songs of love, songs of peace, songs that remember friends long gone. Songs that ride next to your dog on the front seat on the way to your favorite fishing hole, songs that show up unannounced at campfires and stay until the coals are gone. Songs that know how beautiful a place can be because they have seen other places.

Many of Jay's songs are set in Michigan and celebrate its natural beauty. Lakes, woods, rivers...these are their sacred spots and if you are in Michigan on a summer night, at a music festival or campfire, you will hear these songs being sung. They have become part of our state – part of us who live here. And as the words and the melodies waft through the trees, you may forget exactly what year it is because, like all great songs, they are timeless.

Chris Buhalis
Singer-Songwriter

Not Far from Home

Growing up in Ludington, Junior Stielstra – as Jay was known then – was a standout, but not for music and song writing. In that small, west Michigan town it was sports that counted and made heroes out of young boys. Jay broke high school track records that stood for decades, and he excelled in football and basketball. Then, at the University of Michigan in the hard arena of Big Ten sports, Jay proved his athletic fame was not cheaply bought, earning multiple honors and even a medal presented to him by the great Jesse Owens.

By twenty Jay was enveloped in the kind of sports glory that too often stunts talented young men, leaving them confused if not lost when life requires them to move on. Fortunately for all of us, Jay Stielstra was not finished with excellence. He earned accolades for coaching Ann Arbor High football, and then more quietly was known at Ann Arbor's Huron High School as the history and geography teacher who would bring out the best in students judged by others as likely to fail. And then along with the satisfaction of carpentry, he discovered the challenges and fulfillment of writing frankly honest folk songs and folk operas.

Beyond whatever innate talents he was born with, Jay Stielstra had the boon of growing up in a place where kids could reach out and touch nature almost without ever leaving their front yards. With Michigan's most popular state park on the dunes to the north, the mouth of the splendid Pere Marquette River just to the south and east, and the endless horizon of Lake Michigan's waters to the west, it was practically impossible to grow up in Ludington without feeling you were somehow married to the outdoors.

If you know that in Jay's home territory many of the public schools were closed for the first day of hunting season, and fishing was a way of life, you can pretty much figure out the inspiration for a lot of his songwriting. But you don't have be local to northern Michigan to recognize what inspires much of his work. Jay's iconic *Cross Over the Line*, brings a smile to any of us who recall driving along US 10 from Baldwin to Claire and realizing we've just been embraced by forests of jack pine and birch. Those lucky enough to have shared that way of life, get pleasure in recognizing particular points of his songwriting inspiration. I love his recollections in *Boats Came into Ludington*, reminding me of all the Ludington boys who dreamed of getting a summer job that would pay more than their fathers made in a year, shoveling coal on the massive Lake Michigan ferries that swallowed whole trains and made the trip around Chicago unnecessary. And although he may have performed it only once, I have to admit partiality to *The Meat Cutter's Daughter*, Jay's song about me and my family that he was prompted to write for an environmental fundraiser.

Although I too grew up in Ludingtin, I was enough years younger that I could only hold this sports icon in awe. But in the small town we shared we knew each other's families. From his sister I learned Jay's dad was an executive at Ludington's second largest enterprise, Dow Chemical. And as the story was told to me, Jay's family was so religious they couldn't find a suitable church in conspicuously religious Ludington, so they drove south to New Era for their Sunday worshiping.

Jay's real brilliance is his poetry that marries the intimate to the universal. His vehicle for writing of love, the great outdoors, war, religion, or injustice is invariably through the voice of a person who feels just like us, or someone we'd like to know. Jay is not one to accept boundaries of time and age, his songwriting carries us from youth to life's close. Whether he's recalling a hot young infatuation in the *Baker's Daughter* or the longing for just one more gentle touch in *Last Night You Came Alive Again*, the stories have deeply evocative power. In *Liam O'Reilly*, and *Leave the Bottle on the Table, Waiter* Jay has us suffering through war's worst costs; while in *Tittabawassee Jane*, we find ourselves tapping our feet and enjoying the song's humor even as it's impossible not to squirm in hearing "she made napalm ... some kind of bomb...but I wasn't too political then." And in closing the circle of life and death with *Heaven for Me* Jay has us embracing our mortality with a sense of fulfillment as he croons "Buried in the northland, it's God's country."

Up close, we recognize the rich fabric of Jay's young life in his songwriting. And so much of it – his religion reimagined, the tension between Dow's pollution and the company's economic importance in the town he called home, the unpretentious pleasures of smalltown bars embedded in his beloved northern Michigan environment, his barely disguised contempt for puffery masquerading as authority, and of course the memories of past loves – these are all given clear and pure voice in his work. For reasons that only Jay may understand, the glories of his youthful sports fame are not heard in his repetroire. Perhaps it is because Jay Stielstra is quitessentially a modest man, more given to humilitiy than to hubris, more comfortable in the quiet of a trout stream than with the roar of the crowds. His songs are not anthems to a young icon's glory. They are the poetry of a life we'd like to call our own.

Lana Pollack
Michigan Democratic Senator (1983-1994)
President, Michigan Environmental Council (1996-2008)
Chair, US Section, International Joint Commission (2010-2019)

I Love Jay's Songs Because

I love Jay's songs
because they embody
a big-hearted
and meticulous observation
of his fellow human beings

I love Jay's songs
because he traveled with me to Maine
to help build a guest cabin for my parents
and while there, despite the fact that he'd been working hard all day,
spent his evenings
in the bedroom downstairs
writing *Old Man in Love*

I love Jay's songs
because when I asked him when it was we built the cabin in Maine,
he answered, without hesitation: "1987"
and when I asked him, "How did you know that?"
he answered "That's the year Ruby[*] was born" and then chuckling "Ruby…she was the blonde"

I love Jay's songs
because
"hawkweed orange,
hawkweed yellow"
actually pierces my heart
just like an arrow

I love Jay's songs because
I love the man himself

I love Jay's songs
because they're true

I love Jay's songs
because when he sings them
he sings them perfectly in pitch,
his voice resonating with power and feeling

---

[*] Ruby was a yellow Labrador retriever

I love Jay's songs
because they seem simple and easy to sing

but they're not
actually, they are complex
full of melodic nuances
and subtle shifts of meter

I love Jay's songs
because he played a bunch of them at a boisterous 4th of July party in Maine,
(the same Maine where the guest cabin got built)
and successfully transformed a group of raucous revelers into a rapt listening audience
just like he does at the Old Town

I love Jay's songs
because if I'd never heard them
I wouldn't have the friends I've made being in his shows
I wouldn't have played Reggie in *Tittibawassee Jane*
or done a one-night stand as O'Dell in *North Country Opera*
I would never have built with him, hung out, drank beer, talked or sat and said nothing
I would never have known him as the treasured friend he's been for so long

I love Jay's songs
and I wrote a song for him
It's called *Friend's Duet*

Friend's Duet

  Verse
I watch as the sun sinks slow in the west
The earth is a'rollin and I need a rest
I lay my head down and I sing to the wind
That rips at my shutters a song of my friend

  Chorus
You are my friend, my friend you will be
Through the joys and the sorrows of our mystery
In the time that it takes to say thank-you amen
Hallelujah for living and you are my friend

Verse
Love comes in pulses and pounds at the heart
Fixing and breaking and aching apart
Then love leaves in tatters 'til love comes again
Love is just something to speak of with friends

Chorus
You are my friend, my friend you will be
Through the joys and the sorrows of our mystery
In the time that it takes to say thank-you amen
hallelujah for living and you are my friend

Verse
The jungle is a jungle the sea is the sea
You are for you and I am for me
But we're for each other 'cause we can both lend
The pleasure of knowing that you are my friend

Chorus:
You are my friend, my friend yes you are
And the miles don't matter no matter how far
In the time that it takes to say thank-you amen
Hallelujah for living and you are my friend

Chorus:
You are my friend, my friend you will be
Through the joys and the sorrows of our mystery
In the time that it takes to say thank-you amen
Hallelujah for living and you are my friend

Dick Siegel
Singer-Songwriter
Songwriting Instructor – University of Michigan
School of Music, Theater and Dance

A Diamond in Our Midst

I consider Jay Stielstra a founding father of the Ann Arbor music scene.

I first saw him performing at The Ark with John Nordlinger backing him up on piano in the fall of 1968. Don Postema, one of the Ark founders and a member of its board, told me, "You have to come over and see this guy. He's really, really good." Don nailed it. Jay was VERY good. Every song was a gem. One song in particular knocked me out – *Linebacker from Muskegon*, a retelling of the biblical story of the Prodigal Son set in the political unrest of the 1960's. This is simply the best song I've ever heard dealing with the generation gap and the importance of acceptance even when you can't understand.

His songs are direct and simple in structure. His performing style is what I call "living room." It's not geared to overwhelm a big hall; it is intimate. That's not a criticism. Many great songwriters utilize the same style, especially back in the 1960's and 70's – Leonard Cohen, Joni Mitchell, Eric Andersen, and John Prine, to name a few. You listen to every one of Jay's words because every word is there for a reason. I remember listening to John Prine's first album and thinking how similar Jay's songwriting was to his and realizing that Jay was writing at that level; he was as good as anybody out there, including John. They both wrote from their rural roots and they were both great storytellers.

A main difference was that, unlike John, Jay remained local. Like Jay, there are excellent singer/songwriters who preferred to stay in their local areas, who didn't care about national careers. They were well-kept secrets, hidden diamonds, local treasures. Jimmy Dale Gilmore was one of them in Austin until Natalie Merchant took him on tour with her in 1993 and the rest of the country discovered him. Jimmy LaFave was another. They both lived in Austin and were an integral part of the scene there. Jay is one of those diamonds in Michigan. Over the last 50 years, he has created a large body of work of songs and plays about the Michigan woods, the small towns, and the people who live in them. And, in the process of living in Ann Arbor as a coach, a teacher, and a carpenter, he became a mentor for younger songwriters and, without trying, a central figure in the Ann Arbor area music scene from those early days right up to the present. He didn't ask for it; it simply happened. He became a major influence on a whole string of songwriters from Dick Siegel all the way up to Chris Buhalis. There are now many excellent musicians and songwriters that live in and around Ann Arbor forming a very active, connected scene. And in a very real sense, Jay Stielstra deserves much of the credit for it.

When someone wants to know how to write a song, I tell them to listen to Jay – to look at how he structures his songs and how he uses an economy of words to tell his story. He may be little known outside of the state, but I believe he's a very important songwriter from an American perspective and I have no doubt that his work will be lasting. If Michigan were Ireland, I think he'd be declared a National Treasure and given an annual stipend. His songs are classic examples of how profound depth can be achieved in simplicity. If you don't believe me, read them.

Dave Siglin
Director of The Ark, Ann Arbor (1969-2008)

Biography of Jay Stielstra

"Ah, it was a grand life I had…just one big love affair."

So says the title character in the opening monologue of Jay Stielstra's musical play, Old Man in Love, which debuted at the Ark in Ann Arbor in 1988. Old Man in Love is a one-man show in which an old man reminisces about the great loves of his life: the women, the woods and the waters of the Great Lakes country.

The Old Man continues:
> "You see, I figure a person's got so much love to give and you can use it
> up about any way you want… I spent mine on women – and the country
> of the Great Lakes."

In monologues, songs, and poetry, the old man traces the joys and heartbreaks of his past, then faces his own death and the loss of his great loves: waters to pollution, woods and meadows to development, friends and lovers to death.

Still, as Jay describes him, the Old Man is an upbeat character who leaves everyone singing his joyous ode to the state of Michigan, *I'm Singin'*.

Jay played the Old Man at the play's debut when he was only 55, and then seven more times in the years that followed, most recently in 2014 when he was 80. It was the only one of his plays in which he performed, and the role seemed to suit him. He was awarded Best Actor Award by the Ann Arbor News in 1993, and an Annie Award by the Washtenaw Council for the Arts in 1995.

Is *Old Man in Love* autobiographical? Jay says, "to a degree." The similarities are remarkable: Jay and the Old Man shared a very similar upbringing; they both enjoy hunting, fishing and spending time in taverns; both love women and also their dogs. The Old Man muses about the same topics that Jay writes about in his songs, plays, poems and fiction: the beauty of Michigan's northland; love and loss of love; the passage of time; and the folly of war, greed, and environmental destruction.

As a youth, Jay had other interests, most significantly, athletics.

He was born in Holland, Michigan in 1933, and spent most of his childhood years in Midland and Ludington.

Music played only a modest role in his life then. He had minimal formal music education – about nine months of third grade piano lessons, giving him the ability to pick out melodies on a piano.

His first musical influences were Baptist Church hymns. Though Jay soon lost any affinity for religion after learning his dog would not be allowed in heaven, he never lost his fondness for those tunes.

When big band music was popular with his high school classmates, Jay favored the old-style country music of the time – simple tunes played with a handful of instruments and sung by performers like Hank Williams Sr.

Still, his focus was not music then. It was athletics.

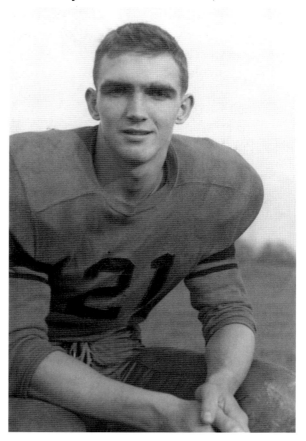

Jay on the Football Field, 1950

Jay was drawn to sports early; he'd been playing basketball in a youth program since he was ten. In high school he began a long string of athletic achievements. He was a track prodigy, very fast, and excelled at the long jump, or broad jump as it was called then. To this day, no other Ludington High School student has ever beat his long jump record (22' 5 3/4").

Recruited on an athletic scholarship to attend the University of Michigan, he played on the football, basketball and track teams, and was the Big Ten Champion in long jump, for which Jesse Owens awarded him the medal.

After graduating, he began his first career in 1955, as a high school teacher and football coach. In 1962, as head coach at Ann Arbor High School – now Pioneer High School – he was named Coach of the Year by the *Detroit News* and *Associated Press* after leading the team to the state championship. He authored the book *Michigan-Style High School Football* in 1969.

His achievements as an athlete and coach would be later recognized with inductions into the Mason County Sports Hall of Fame in 2010 and the Michigan High School Football Association Coaches Hall of Fame in 2014.

In the 1960s and 70s, he diverted his attention to social activism, visiting the north, and songwriting.

Jay remained in Ann Arbor over the next several decades, where his three children were born.

He taught Social Studies and American History in the Ann Arbor public schools from 1956-1986, during key years in the civil rights era. He attended summer courses at Spelman College, the traditionally black liberal arts school in Atlanta, and became one of two teachers responsible for creating guidelines to integrate black history into the standard American History curriculum in Ann Arbor. He also taught the first high school course dedicated to black history.

Jay's lessons made lasting impressions on his students, many of whom who would go on to distinguished careers with local, national and international impact; they include award winning journalists, educators, activists, philanthropists, artists, entrepreneurs, and a professional Elvis impersonator.

He ran for Ann Arbor city council in 1964 ("Public apathy is our worst enemy"), was a board member of the local chapter of the American Civil Liberties Union, and marched in Washington DC in 1969 to protest the war in Viet Nam.

Around 1960, he bought a $19 guitar so he could sing children's songs to his two young daughters. He taught himself basic guitar chords from an instructional manual and says now that, as a guitar player, he's never advanced beyond that point.

He began writing his own songs in the mid-1960s, influenced by the folk musicians of that time, such as Pete Seeger and the Kingston Trio. He would describe his music as "old-style" country: simple chords, simple arrangements.

Jay Teaching in the 1960s

A Student Recollection

"My first class my first hour of my first year at Huron High School in 1972 was taught by Jay Stielstra.

He arrived that first morning dressed in casual clothes and parked himself in the midst of class rather than taking a traditional stand up front. His topic was the commentary he'd heard watching a Michigan football game over the weekend and how the announcer described the "Good Ol' American Names" on the team's roster.

He cautioned us about ever drawing conclusions about anyone based on their ethnicity and suggested we discard our preconceived notions about anyone and reserve judgement until we'd actually met them.

Jay Stielstra was unlike any teacher I ever had. His objective was to prepare us for life, not test us on what we memorized. Some 45 years after I was in his class, he still remembers my name. I don't think I'll ever forget his."

Peter Stipe

Excerpted from March 7, 2017 post on: https://www.facebook.com/groups/AnnArborTownies/

He had also begun to explore the northern parts of the state, after Black, his first Labrador Retriever, joined his family. Jay's friends suggested he take her bird hunting and he soon treasured the camaraderie he developed with her. They frequently joined his friends in exploring the northern woods, looking for upland game birds and fishing trout in cold northern streams.

He built a "shack" up north – a humble but livable structure that was part launching site for bird hunting and trout fishing excursions, and part retreat from modern amenities.

His appreciation for the beauty of northern Michigan was becoming a regular theme in his growing song repertoire, joining songs about the devastation of war, finding and losing love, drinking in taverns, and getting old.

Jay's first public performance was in 1973. He sang *Grosse Pointe Wins Again* with his "wretched old guitar" at an open mic night at The Ark, located then on Hill Street. Soon thereafter, with the new Guild guitar he still plays today, he was performing regularly at Mr. Flood's Party, a beloved townie bar, sometimes accompanied by John Nordlinger, a piano player and fellow high school teacher.

April 1977 Calendar for Mr. Flood's Party, Showing Jay Stielstra Scheduled for Both the 3rd and the 25th of the Month

He remained athletic, playing competitive basketball with the Ann Arbor City League throughout his 30s and 40s, and continuing to play pickup games well into his 70s.

Jay wrote his first play, *North Country Opera*, in 1982.

It was a musical play, set it in a bar in northern Michigan. Jay focused the plot around a love story, and populated it with characters that hunted, fished and drank beer. He cast some of the singers he met at Mr. Flood's and other venues.

North Country Opera was the second play staged at the Performance Network and it was immediately and tremendously popular. The cast and crew took the production on a tour of northern Michigan and the UP, and reprised their roles several more times over the next quarter century.

Encouraged by the success of *North Country Opera*, Jay went on to write a number of plays, mostly musicals, in the next decade: *The Prodigals* (1983), *Tittabawassee Jane* (1984), *Old Man in Love* (1988), *America, America* (1992), and the non-musical, *A Better Way to Die* (1995). He wrote *North Country Opera Continued*, a sequel, in 2003. All were well reviewed.

Jay's reputation as a songwriter and playwright widened. Music or theater writers referred to Jay as "a folk tunesmith – surely one of the best our state has ever produced," a "Michigan's poet laureate" and a "Michigan Treasure." The lyrics to the title song from *Tittabawassee Jane* were featured on the front page of the Washington Post in 1983, to accompany an article about Dow Chemical.

He became a regular performer at music venues throughout Michigan and was invited to music festivals in other states. His bands from that time, the McDonald Brothers and then the Country Quartet, featured fiddle, piano, guitar, bass and sometimes drums.

Jay Stielstra Trio: Judy Banker, John Sayler and Jay

He dabbled a little more in acting, playing Virgil in Detroit's Attic Theater's production of *Bus Stop*, and was an understudy in *Hot L Baltimore* at Chelsea's Purple Rose Theater.

After retiring from teaching, he'd started another career building houses full-time, a trade he'd once pursued in summers between school years. One of the houses he built was in Maine. Another was on Inish Bofin, an island off the west coast of Ireland. After shortening the middle finger of his left hand in a mishap with a table saw in 2009, he took some time off from performing.

He began performing again with his friends, John Sayler and Judy Banker, as the Jay Stielstra Trio. When John passed in 2012, Jay continued his musical partnership with Judy, who continues to sing with him and produce his musical projects.

"Now I am an Old Man"

Jay was in his early 50s when he wrote his song, *Hey Buddy, It's Still Me*, so it took decades for his lyrics to catch up with him. When he sings it, he still delivers the last words as he always has, vigorously and joyfully:

> "Now I am an old man, I dream an old man's dreams
> No longer hunt the low land or fish the brushy streams
> My body's but a costume now, well weathered you can see
> Still here inside this disguise, hey buddy, it's still me"

And indeed, it's still him.

Jay lives with me in the country outside Ann Arbor, and more often than not, a Labrador Retriever has kept us company. He continues to go north, to the shack or the U.P., though he doesn't hunt or fish much.

He tinkers with an unpublished novel and an unproduced play. And he still plays music occasionally, expressing gratitude for Judy and the other musical friends who perform with him.

In 2017, the State of Michigan honored Jay with a Legislative Tribute, after a longtime conservationist and supporter of acoustic music, Mary Sexton, and Senator Rebekah Warren, proposed the idea to the state's legislature. The Tribute recognizes Jay's "countless artistic accomplishments and profound appreciation for the state of Michigan… His songs, musicals, and poems are timeless, reflecting a deep admiration for the natural wonders of our great state, and will undoubtedly leave a lasting impression well into the future."

> "Thanks to all for coming out tonight and hearing an old man sing. You buy me a drink and I'll tell you a story. Tell you one even if you don't. It was a grand life I had." (From the Old Man's closing monologue)

Barbara Schmid

"A Michigan Tribute to Jay Stielstra," The Ark, 2017
Performers Ask Jay to Lead the Final Song of the Night – I'm Singing

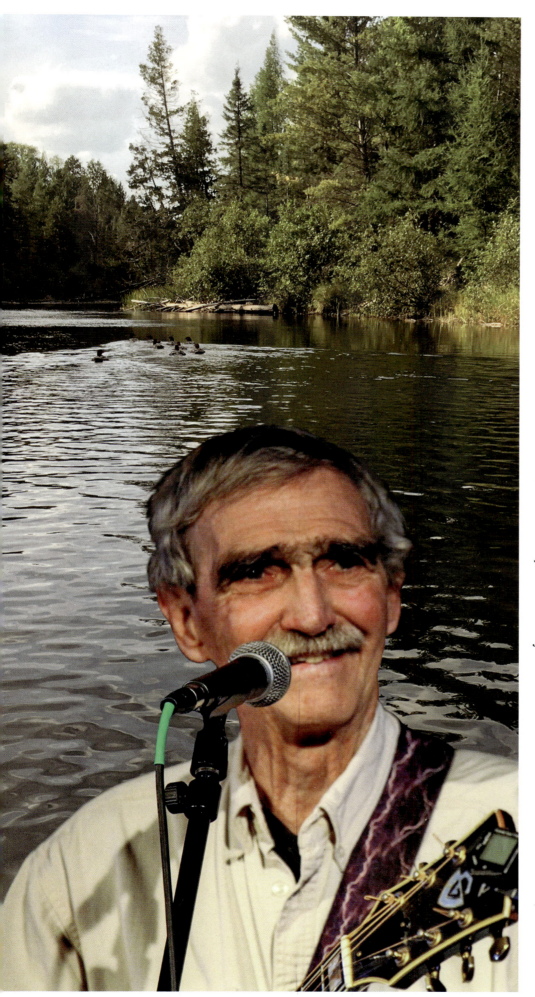

Heaven for Me

Playing music with Jay has given me some of the best musical experiences I've ever had, times I cherish – rooms filled with voices joining in on I'm Singin', *Jay's Michigan anthem, or the feeling of collective heartache when we perform the* Manistee Waltz, *Jay's ode to fallen friends. That is the magic of Jay's music – it evokes our treasured memories while creating shared memories to hold.*

  Judy Banker, Singer-Songwriter, Jay's singing partner and music producer since 2009

Road Less Traveled

I took the road less traveled back when I was young
Never walked away, I never bit my tongue
Some would call me cocky then, tough as I could be
But freedom was the only word worth a damn to me

    I took the road less traveled, not the one that's paved
    I took the road less traveled, I thought I was so brave
    No one to navigate me, no one to count the cost
    I took the road less traveled and now I'm really lost

  I should've had a compass, I should've had a guide
  Some one that I trusted to travel by my side

I know I said I love you to women that I found
A few when standing up, more when lying down
They all tried to change me, make me someone else
And I can't say I blame them when I look at myself

    I took the road less traveled, not the one that's paved
    I took the road less traveled, I thought I was so brave
    No one to navigate me, no one to count the cost
    I took the road less traveled and now I'm really lost

I coulda took the broad way, well lit and straight to hell
But I found that my way got me there as well
It really doesn't matter, I'm sorry Mr. Frost
I took your road less traveled and all I got was lost

    I took the road less traveled, not the one that's paved
    I took the road less traveled, I thought I was so brave
    No one to navigate me, no one to count the cost
    I took the road less traveled and now I'm really lost

Road Less Traveled

Going Home

I'm going home to the golden meadow
Hawkweed orange and hawkweed yellow
I'm going home where the white birch stands
In the jackpine hills of northern Michigan

I come down when I was young
Fancy words upon my tongue
Fancy thoughts inside my mind
Any fool could tell I left my soul behind

I passed right on by Traverse City
Took a job outside Detroit
Thought that I'd be sitting pretty
Bought a girl to share the night

Spent my evenings getting high
Spent my mornings getting well
There was nothing I wouldn't buy
There was nothing I wouldn't sell

Now I'm going home to the golden meadow
Hawkweed orange and hawkweed yellow
I'm going home where the white birch stands
In the jackpine hills of northern Michigan

Light a cigar of fine tobacco
Let the wail of the coyote echo
Let the call of the white-throat sparrow
Pierce my ear just like an arrow

Jay's Cabin and His Dog Maggie in Northern Michigan

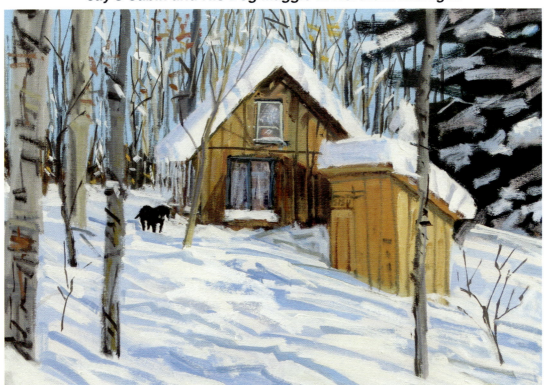

Going Home

Cross Over the Line

Beyond the drains on the Bay City plains
By fields of tomatoes and beets
There is a line not that hard to find
Where the south and the northland meet
You'll know you're there from Baldwin to Clare
See the white birches and pines
Lakes as blue as turquoise jewels
You know you crossed over the line

    You know you crossed over the line
    Really not that hard to find
    See the white birches and pines
    You know you crossed over the line

For no good reason there's only three seasons
The winter, the summer, the fall
Spring's but a day come late in May
'Tween mosquitoes and the last snowfall
More white-tail deer than people up here
Morels though quite hard to find
Black flies in the air and some in your hair
You know you crossed over the line

    You know you crossed over the line
    Really not that hard to find
    See the white birches and pines
    You know you crossed over the line

There is a strait of two Great Lakes
There's a magnificent bridge
You'll know the place by the look on my face
And spruce on the far north ridge
The soil's no good for nothing but wood
Maybe grapes for a so-so wine
Look down where you stand, see nothing but sand
You know you crossed over the line

    You know you crossed over the line
    Really not that hard to find
    See the white birches and pines
    You know you crossed over the line

White Birches, Keweenaw, MI

Cross Over the Line

I'm Singing

I love it in the summer, I love it in the fall
Wintertime and springtime, Lord I love them all
Let me say to you when's all done and said
I know that I will love it even when I'm dead

    I'm singing, I'm singing 'bout this old State of mine
    Closest thing to heaven that I will ever find
    Her Great Lakes and her rivers are flowing sweet as wine
    And an old empty beer can can buy a man a dime

I fished her icy rivers with every kind of fly
Shot straight at the partridge though most refused to die
I skied her silent forests, seen chickadees at play
And hunted magic mushrooms some secret place in May

    I'm singing, I'm singing 'bout this old State of mine
    Closest thing to heaven that I will ever find
    Her Great Lakes and her rivers are flowing sweet as wine
    And an old empty beer can can buy a man a dime

 I love those April mornings when spring is finally here
And evenings late in June filled with mayflies and beer
How I love October with leaves of polished brass
And even January with the snow up to my ass

    I'm singing, I'm singing 'bout this old State of mine
    Closest thing to heaven that I will ever find
    Her Great Lakes and her rivers are flowing sweet as wine
    And an old empty beer can can buy a man a dime

I woke November mornings, hung over, oh my God
Sat out on a deer stand where countless bucks have trod
Cursing bourbon whiskey and the day that I was born
From early light to late at night and never saw a horn

    I'm singing, I'm singing 'bout this old State of mine
    Closest thing to heaven that I will ever find
    Her Great Lakes and her rivers are flowing sweet as wine
    And an old empty beer can can buy a man a dime

Now I hate mosquitoes, black flies are even worse
The flies of Lake Superior are the very devil's curse
But when you take the bitter and mix it with the sweet
Down it goes with a can of Strohs, oh lord, it can't be beat

    I'm singing, I'm singing 'bout this old State of mine
    Closest thing to heaven that I will ever find
    Her Great Lakes and her rivers are flowing sweet as wine
    And an old empty beer can can buy a man a dime

I'm Singing

Never Been Much of a Ramblin' Man

    Never been much of a ramblin' man
    Doin' about as well as I can
    Born and raised in Michigan
    Never been much of a ramblin' man

Snow upon the mountain tops, salt in the sea they say
Some are born to wander, Lord, some are born to stay

    So I never been much of a ramblin' man
    Doin' about as well as I can
    Born and raised in Michigan
    Never been much of a ramblin' man

I drank too much, I bragged too much, lived a bit too free
Hangin' 'round this old town may be the death of me

    But I never been much of a ramblin' man
    Doin' about as well as I can
    Born and raised in Michigan
    Never been much of a ramblin' man

Walked the streams where the steelhead run
Stalked the pats with an old shotgun
Had me some trouble and a whole lot of fun
Have me some more before I'm done

    But I never been much of a ramblin' man
    Doin' about as well as I can
    Born and raised in Michigan
    Never been much of a ramblin' man

Snow upon the mountain tops, salt in the sea they say
Some are born to wander, Lord, some are born to stay

    Some are born to wander, Lord, some are born to stay

Never Been Much of a Ramblin' Man

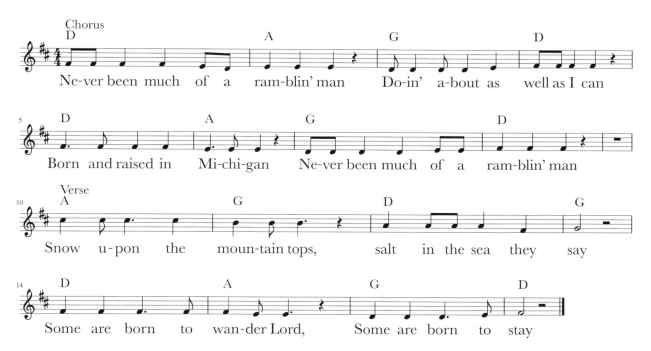

Manistee Waltz

Will the whippoorwill call by the river tonight
And the big trout rise for the fly
Will old friends gather in the campfire light
As we have in the years gone by

Will we talk small as we always have done
And pretend to change not a thing
Will one of us there strum a guitar
Pick out a song and sing

> The Manistee River runs through Deward
> And the Manistee runs through Sharon
> She flows, I know, when we're thinking out loud
> And she flows when nobody's caring

Will she run clear as Stolichnaya
From Yellow Trees to the Ranch
Will the beer stay cold in the Mecum Bar
When the mayflies rise to dance

Will the weather be as unpredictable?
And the fishing as well the same
Will we carry on as we've always done
And scarcely mention his name

> The Manistee River runs through Deward
> And the Manistee runs through Sharon
> She flows, I know, when we're thinking out loud
> And she flows when nobody's caring

Will a solitary mink hunt on her bank
And the coyote sing out tonight
Will bank beavers gather at their favorite holes
In the warm June's late twilight

Will the Manistee River give us a nod
To tell us that she really knows
We're weaker and fewer this year by one
And trying to not let it show

    The Manistee River runs through Deward
    And the Manistee runs through Sharon
    She flows, I know, when we're thinking out loud
    And she flows when nobody's caring

The Manistee River Near Deward, MI

Manistee Waltz

Black River Jones

Black River Black River you're cold and you're clean
Like a trickle from God's ice-making machine
Often you're running as deep as you're wide
With many dark places for beauty to hide

    I know you old river, you're a witch and a shrew
    You promised so many and favored so few
    I love you Black River, your pockets and stones
    You left me forever with the Black River jones

The beaver, the brook trout, they live there you know
The elk and the bobcat drink from your flow
The color of walnut or mahogany stain
Fed through the swamp from yesterday's rain

    I know you old river, you're a witch and a shrew
    You promised so many and favored so few
    I love you Black River, your pockets and stones
    You left me forever with the Black River jones

I waded through muck and across stone beds
I fought the tag alder and canoed the spreads
Your little brook trout I caught by the score
And cursed when I lost one of thirteen or more

    I know you old river, you're a witch and a shrew
    You promised so many and favored so few
    I love you Black River, your pockets and stones
    You left me forever with the Black River jones

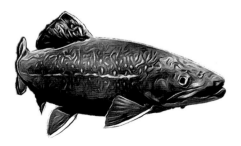

Black River Jones

Boats Came into Ludington

I understand in New England young men are drawn to sea
Also I know that long ago it was the same for me
The boats came into Ludington when I was just a boy
They came out from Manitowoc and down by Charlevoix

    We dreamed of when we'd be men and work upon the boats
    We'd all be skippers on the bridge with braid upon our coats
    We ended up as stokers in the part that barely floats

A whistle blew, one of the crew cast away the line
There was nothing to it in the sun of summertime
In wintertime the winch'd whine, the wind blew ice and cold
Then a man could lose a hand if he were too bold

We bore it well, our time in hell, we called it a career
Soon we'd be in Milwaukee and drink our fill of beer
I sailed with Stanley Gutchke there, two teeth inside his head
For forty years he drank his meals and still he is not dead

Four hours on, eight hours off, for twenty days and then
Eight days ashore, all whored and bored, and back we'd go again
The boats came into Ludington when I was just a boy
They came out from Manitowoc and down by Charlevoix

Boats Came into Ludington

ERRATUM

One verse of the following song was inadvertently omitted in printing. The full lyrics are below.

Boats Came into Ludington

I understand in New England young men are drawn to sea
Also I know that long ago it was the same for me
The boats came into Ludington when I was just a boy
They came out from Manitowoc and down by Charlevoix

    We dreamed of when we'd be men and work upon the boats
    We'd all be skippers on the bridge with braid upon our coats
    We ended up as stokers in the part that barely floats

A whistle blew, one of the crew cast away the line
There was nothing to it in the sun of summertime
In wintertime the winch'd whine, the wind blew ice and cold
Then a man could lose a hand if he were too bold

At eighteen years, you have no fears
None but yourself to please
A ship ashore, astern, afore, to windward or to lee
Storms out there can strip you bare, and bring you to your knees

We bore it well, our time in hell, we called it a career
Soon we'd be in Milwaukee and drink our fill of beer
I sailed with Stanley Gutchke there, two teeth inside his head
For forty years he drank his meals and still he is not dead

Four hours on, eight hours off, for twenty days and then
Eight days ashore, all whored and bored, and back we'd go again
The boats came into Ludington when I was just a boy
They came out from Manitowoc and down by Charlevoix

The Lake

Some come to bask on the beach by day
Some to make love when the sun sinks away
Some come in quest of the fish by the pier
The Lake infatuates in the warm of the year

    But you can't begin to know it 'til you've seen it in November
    When the breakwall disappears and the waves have turned to thunder
    It doesn't roll, it thrashes and you shudder at its anger
    No colors blossom on its beach, no lovers sit upon its lap
    And a man is but a cricket you remember

Mothers bring their babies to the shore in June
To play in the sand with a pail and a spoon
They take off their shoes and most of their clothes
And giggle at the tickle of the Lake on their toes

    But you can't begin to know it 'til the month of January
    When there is no beach at all 'cause the icebergs have it buried
    Only fools and suicides dare risk its fury
    One can't even dream of spring, such an odd and distant thing
    There is naught to do but fret and worry

Lake Huron in January 2018

They shoot fireworks on the Fourth of July
Up from the sand to the fat purple sky
Crowds on the beach they cheer and they clap
The Lake sleeps calm as a kitten in your lap

    But you can't begin to know it 'til you've seen the front come in
    Always late in August to mark the summer's end
    And bring a grim reminder of who we are and when
    It closes down the fine resorts, locks the yachters in the ports
    And a man is but a cricket once again

She's pretty as a woman and big as the sky
Angry as God in a churchgoer's eye
She'll float a boat 'til it's nearly home
Then let it sink like a granite gray stone

    She'll float a boat 'til it's nearly home
    Then let it sink like a granite gray stone

Jay and Maggie Strolling on Lake Michigan Beach, U.P. 2014

Great Lakes Storm Coming

The Lake

Cut River Bridge

You want to see something you'll never forget
It's in the U.P. up near Epofette
On October 10 it'll turn all your heads
Stop for a view from the Cut River Bridge

    They say in New Hampshire, they say in Vermont
    The colors are lovely, what more could you want

    Well I been to the Louvre, I been to the Prado
    And I seen real Van Goghs, I seen real Picasso
    But I never seen such shining bright reds
    As the leaves of October from the Cut River Bridge

I seen fireworks on the Fourth of July
Fountains of light shot up in the sky
But nothing compares to the valley and ridge
Seen October 10 from the Cut River Bridge

    One hundred fifty feet down below
    Runs the Cut River, now lost in the show

    Well I been to the Louvre, I been to the Prado
    And I seen real Van Gohs, I seen real Picasso
    But I never seen such shining bright reds
    As the leaves of October from the Cut River Bridge

Cut River Bridge, Cut River Bridge
There's people with dogs and people with kids
All looking out at the valley and ridge
It's October 10 on the Cut River Bridge

Cut River Bridge

Heaven for Me

I was just a young man, the preacher said to me
Time to give some thought, boy, to eternity
Where will you go when the final trumpet sounds
Will you go up or will you go down

    I said, Preacher, don't you know, I thought by now you'd learned
    We all come from dust and to dust we shall return
    And heaven for me, yeah, heaven for me
    Is buried in the northland, it's God's country

You see I've been to heaven I've seen the other shore
Starts down by Roscommon, goes a thousand miles more
So you can save your preaching and you can save your prayers
When I cross the big Mac bridge I climb the golden stairs

    And oh that will be Heaven for me
    Heaven for me, yeah, heaven for me
    Oh that will be heaven for me
    Buried in the northland, it's God's country

So hand me down my fly rod and hand me down my gun
Dress me in my waders when my days on earth are done
Dump me in some corner in northern Michigan
Wrap my stiffened fingers 'round a Pabst Blue Ribbon can

    And oh that will be Heaven for me
    Heaven for me, yeah, heaven for me
    Oh that will be heaven for me
    Buried in the northland, it's God's country

Mackinac Bridge

Heaven for Me

Memories to Hold

(Stielstra's songs)…are a gift of magic from a guy whose heart is as big as North Country, and who writes songs that people swear have been around for 100 years.

Jim Moran, Producer of Stielstra's musical *North Country Opera*

Baker's Daughter

She was the baker's daughter
I'll not reveal her name
But since I bought a pastry there
I've never been the same

Buns, you bet she had 'em, boys
Oven warm and sweet
And loaves to rock a baby on
Good enough to eat

   Frostings so delicious, cream to golden tan
   If I can't have a piece of cake, least let me lick the pan

   She was the baker's daughter
   I'll not reveal her name
   But since I bought a pastry there
   I've never been the same

Now I dream of raspberries
Rosy, red and grand
Decorating rolls that rise
Curved to fit my hand

   Though it happened long ago, the memory's not erased
   Of that oh so sweet tart, the texture and the taste

   She was the baker's daughter
   I'll not reveal her name
   But since I bought a pastry there
   I've never been the same

Jay's Story:
   She was two years older than me and beautiful. Her father was a baker and she worked in his shop. We teenagers often gathered there to tease and beg for an occasional free pastry. Fifty years later I wrote this song.
   Not long after that I ran into her sister at a class reunion. I didn't mention the song but did say that we all thought her sister was so beautiful.
   "Oh, she was!" said her sister, or "Oh, she still is!" I forget which.

Baker's Daughter

November Love

The days grow short, the leaves are down
A morning frost lies on the ground
The wind blows chill, gray clouds above
I dream of you, November Love

    Won't you come back and hold me one more time
    Pretend I'm yours and you are mine
    The tune plays slow, the words in rhyme
    Won't you come back and hold me one more time

The days and weeks turn into years
The winds of time have dried my tears
So long ago when we first met
November Love, I can't forget

    Won't you come back and hold me one more time
    Pretend I'm yours and you are mine
    The tune plays slow, the words in rhyme
    Won't you come back and hold me one more time

November Love

Wednesday's Child

Driftwood haired, a little scared, not enough to make it known
She came to me like a melody and slipped inside my bones
How was I to know, buck young and running wild
Though fair of face and blessed with grace, she was Wednesday's child

The years they passed like hurricanes, few days were fair and mild
She could not change her destiny of being Wednesday's child
I loved her then back in those times, though she tore my heart in two
I don't believe in nursery rhymes, it may not be true

That Monday's child is fair of face and Tuesday's child is blessed with grace
But Wednesday's child I'm sure it's so, Wednesday's child is filled with woe

    Thursday's child she could not be, not Friday's child or Saturday's
    She was not blessed more than the rest and could not be of the Sabbath day

Oh, Monday's child is fair of face and Tuesday's child is blessed with grace
But Wednesday's child, though I loved her so, Wednesday's child is filled with woe

Wednesday's Child

I Love Two Rivers and Only One Woman

I love two rivers and only one woman
They mean more than life to me
I'll never tell you the name of the woman
The rivers are the Fox and the Manistee

    All you fishers of trout the world over
    Know the value of what I have said
    For a man never tells you the rivers he fishes
    Unless he loves someone more instead

We waded those rivers right side by side
Took our share on the flies that we tied
We fished in the glare of the noon-day sun
Where the tag alder touches at the tops of the runs

    All you fishers of trout the world over
    Know the value of what I have said
    For a man never tells you the rivers he fishes
    Unless he loves someone more instead

We camped on the edge of a blueberry patch
Waited for dark and the mayfly hatch
We fished the black water where the river runs deep
And lay tangled together at night when we'd sleep

    I love two rivers and only one woman
    They mean more than life to me
    I'll never tell you the name of the woman
    The rivers are the Fox and the Manistee

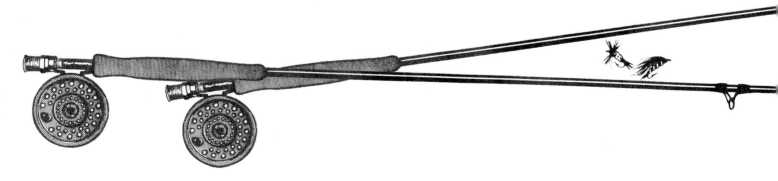

I Love Two Rivers and Only One Woman

I love two rivers and on-ly one wo-man They mean more than li-fe to me (and) I'll ne-ver tell you the name of the wo-man The ri-vers are the Fox and the Ma-ni-stee All you fish-ers of trout the world o-ver Know the val-ue of what I have said For a man ne-ver tells you the ri-vers he fish-es Un-less he loves some-one mo-re in-stead

So Easy

So easy to say you love me tonight
So easy to stay by my side
So easy to play it's all okay
Pretend we got nothing to hide

So easy to come here for a whirl
Bury our cares inside
So easy to run away from the world
Leave all our troubles behind

    So easy, so easy, what more can I say
    Seems like tomorrow is so far away

So easy to love you, so easy to dream
A rainbow, a pot of gold
With the rise of the sun it's all over and done
And I've only a memory to hold

So Easy

Fragile Thing

Love is such a fragile thing
Like a wine glass for a king
Ephemeral as a mayfly wing
Love is such a fragile thing

Here today, tomorrow gone
Someone left so all alone
Without a wave, without a song
Here today, tomorrow gone

   Love can be a whisper
   Love can be a shout
   It can let you in
   It can shut you out

And there's no warning on the door
Turn the knob, the risk is yours
No way to know what you're in for
There's no warning on the door

Love is such a fragile thing
Like a wine glass for a king
Ephemeral as a mayfly wing
Love is such a fragile thing

Fragile Thing

Times That We Had

When my pictures are all long gone from the wall
And I'm just a name from the past
Might there still be a part way back in your heart
That remembers the times that we had

      Remembers the times that we had, love
      Remembers the times that we had
      Might there still be a part way back in your heart
      That remembers the times that we had

In the late twilight of a warm June night
When there's a hum in the breeze
Will the stark silhouettes of the trees in the west
Somehow remind you of me

And when you walk the bank of my favorite river
And see a may fly in the air
Will you think of the times we had together
And remember the love that we shared

When you found another to pass out your days
And keep you from lonely and sad
Every once in a while with a slip of a smile
Will you remember the times that we had

      Remember the times that we had, love
      Remember the times that we had
      Every once in a while with a slip of a smile
      Will you remember the times that we had

Times That We Had

I'll Remember

Of the memories that we have, most are either good or bad
Those in between pass on by
But the dreams that were broken, the lines that went unspoken
These I'll remember 'till I die

There were women that I knew, especially one or two
That hurt me so I almost lost my mind
There were others I forgot right there on the spot
And one I'll remember 'till I die

> I'll remember, I'll remember, 'till I die, 'till I die
> One I'll remember 'till I die

There were picnics on the ground with morels that we found
And trout that we'd taken on the fly
There were plans that were laid, loves that were made
Times I'll remember 'till I die

But once when I was stuck, all down upon my luck
And thought a certain call would ease my time
She said she couldn't chat, asked if she could call me back
I'll remember, I'll remember 'till I die

> I'll remember, I'll remember, 'till I die, 'till I die
> Lord, I'll remember 'till I die

I'll Remember

Don't Let Me Down Easy

Don't let me down easy, keep me hangin' out there
If you really are leavin', if you no longer care
For the sooner I know, babe, the sooner I heal
Don't let me down easy, tell me right how you feel

There once was a time, love, we trembled inside
The thought of us parting put a tear in your eye
Now if it's all over and you're goin' away
Don't let me down easy, say what you gotta say

    Don't let me down easy 'cause my heart's gonna break
    Don't let me down easy for the old time's sake

Don't tell me you're sorry, that we still can be friends
Don't say that someday we may meet again
If you really are goin', my world's gonna fall
Don't let me down easy, just tell me, that's all

Don't Let Me Down Easy

Last Night You Came Alive Again

Last night you came alive again, but the vision did not last
I saw you by my side again though several years had passed
I wonder how you look today, is your hair still dark and long
I wonder do you laugh as much, my memory's not too strong

I'd like to hold your hand again, feel your gentle touch
But I doubt if I could stand again to be in love that much
Time, it does some funny things, it washed away your face
But last night you came alive again and filled an empty place

I try recalling how I felt when I held you in my arms
My mind it wanders to someone else with only half your charms
Pleasure lasts a little while, pain will always be
But last night you came alive again and spent some time with me

Last Night You Came Alive Again

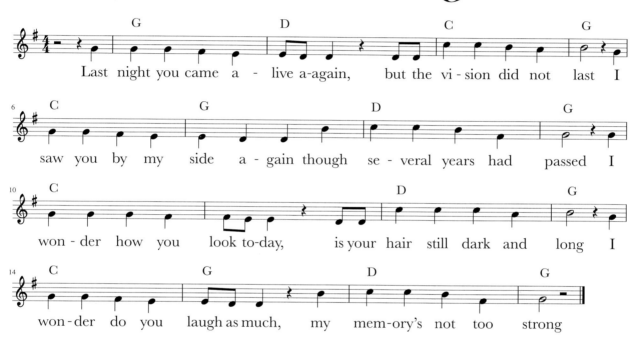

Far Side of the Bed

Ah, she was a lovely bride, I never will forget
The lovelight in her eyes, I can see it yet
We had lots of babies, 'course now they're all grown
And we seldom got together 'til her passing brought 'em home

We took her to a place we'd never been before
And I can't take her home with me anymore
And the far side of the bed is as cold as a stone
I just can't get used to sleeping alone

I'm not quite the man I was a while ago
The last two three years I been moving kinda slow
Then she slipped away, with no warning she was gone
Like the evening star with the coming of the dawn

    And the far side of the bed is as cold as a stone
    I just can't get used to sleeping alone

Far Side of the Bed

Darlin' Except You

Got a fire in the woodstove, good dog at my feet
A twelve pack in the icebox and all I want to eat
Got a full tank in my pickup, some cash on me too
I got everything I want, darlin', except you

My house is snug and dry, got some good books on the shelf
Though the years have slipped on by I been lucky with my health
Friends I got so many I scarce know what to do
I got everything I want, darlin', except you

    Darlin', except you, darlin', except you
    I got everything I want, darlin', except you

Got a flyrod and a shotgun, one good old guitar
Some days I walk the woodland, some nights I play the bars
My good times been so many, my bad times been so few
I got everything I want, darlin', except you

    Darlin', except you, darlin', except you
    I got everything I want, darlin', except you

Darlin' Except You

Lord, What Do We Know

I walked by the river on an old familiar lane
Overgrown by a summer of plentiful rain
'Till I came to the beech tree still standing there
And the ivy around it, three leaves, oh beware

    There were our initials carved in the bark
    An arrow through the middle and around them a heart
    We never dreamed that we'd ever part
    Lord, what do we know

Is love a river bubbling on by
Changing as often as clouds in the sky
Or is it a beech tree sturdy and sound
Lasting a lifetime with roots in the ground

    For there were our initials carved in the bark
    An arrow through the middle and around them a heart
    We never dreamed that we'd ever part
    Lord, what do we know

The ivy around it, oh we should have guessed
Love is a gamble and life is a test
One day we're carving our heart on a tree
The next day we're scratching the itch to be free

    But for there were our initials carved in the bark
    An arrow through the middle and around them a heart
    We never dreamed that we'd ever part
    Lord, what do we know

Lord, What Do We Know

Most I'm Missing You

I'm missing northern waters, we traveled by canoe
I even miss mosquitoes and portages we went through
I'm missing a bald eagle or moose around the bend
We glided soft away, not wanting to offend
I'm missing the big Lake when the sky was blue
But of all that I'm missing, the most I'm missing you

    The most I'm missing you, the most I'm missing you
    Of all that I'm missing, the most I'm missing you

I'm missing hunting partridge with the dogs in the fall
Black, Bido, Chloe, Ruby, Lord, I miss 'em all
I miss skiing in the forest when the snow was new
And finding spring morels some places that we knew
I'm missing the cold rivers, brook trout I took a few
But of all that I'm missing, the most I'm missing you

    The most I'm missing you, the most I'm missing you
    Of all that I'm missing, the most I'm missing you

Red Rose

Barbara's Waltz

I was dancing with Barbara on a warm summer night
By the light of a nearly full moon
She was my darlin', what wonderful sight
Sweet as the air at twilight in June

    I was dancing with Barbara in my own clumsy way
    I skipped and I tripped a fantastic display
    Some people there shook their heads in dismay
    But I was dancing with Barbara, what more can I say

I was dancing with Barbara a one-two-three waltz
She said she'd have me in spite of my faults
We were dancing as if no others were there
We were dancing, we were dancing in the soft summer air

    I was dancing with Barbara in my own clumsy way
    I skipped and I tripped a fantastic display
    Some people there shook their heads in dismay
    But I was dancing with Barbara, what more can I say

Now I've danced with others outdoors in June
In December inside some familiar saloon
Those I've forgotten with a toss of my head
But this I'll remember until I am dead

    I was dancing with Barbara in my own clumsy way
    I skipped and I tripped a fantastic display
    Some people there shook their heads in dismay
    But I was dancing with Barbara, what more can I say

Barbara's Waltz

It's a Wonder

It's a wonder the stars, how they twinkle at night
And the moon sheds its pale yellow glow on the land
It's a wonder the sun shines so warm and bright
It's a wonder I will never understand

It's a wonder the wind never ceases to blow
And the waves roll in upon the shore
It's a wonder the birds know right where to go
It's a wonder, it's a wonder, it's a wonder

> But the greatest wonder that I'll ever see
> As the years, they slip slowly by
> Is the wonder of you still loving me
> It's a wonder, it's a wonder, it's a wonder

It's a wonder the streams wash clean in the spring
And the trout rise up to the fly
It's a wonder to me the joy that it brings
It's a wonder, may I never reason why

It's a wonder the woods turn gold in the fall
And the birds flush up to the sky
It's a wonder for no one deserves it at all
It's a wonder, it's a wonder, it's a wonder

> But the greatest wonder that I'll ever see
> As the years, they slip slowly by
> Is the wonder of you still loving me
> It's a wonder, it's a wonder, it's a wonder

Hands of Time

Singing Jay's songs is effortless; his words and music timeless and exquisitely paired. Years later, a lyric comes to mind or a melody rolls off your lips — and there you are, the song returning to you as an old friend or flame, like no time has passed at all.

Tracy Leigh Komarmy Jaffe, Singer and Actress, Sari in *North Country Opera*, 1992, and *North Country Opera Continued*, 2003, Meg in *A Better Way to Die*, 1995, Jane in *Tittabawassee Jane*, 2010

Hands of Time

You can roll in the hay, you can roll in the clover
Roll on your back and turn yourself over
Roll a drunk in a dark alley
Roll on Columbia down to the sea
You can roll and rock and roll up the points
Roll out the barrel or roll yourself a joint
Roll out the carpet red as wine
But you can't roll back the hands of time

    No, you can't roll back the hands of time
    You can't roll back the hands of time
    Roll out the carpet red as wine
    But you can't roll back the hands of time

You can turn the corner, you can turn the page
Turn white-headed in your ripe old age
Turn in bed and toss as well
Turn to Jesus if you're scared of hell
Turn on the radio, play yourself a song
Turn on the lights or just turn on
Turn on your friends, turn on a dime
But you can't turn back the hands of time

    You can't turn back the hands of time
    You can't turn back the hands of time
    Turn on your friends, turn on a dime
    But you can't turn back the hands of time

You can walk your dog, you can walk your cat
Walk yourself and lose some fat
Walk because your car ain't new
Walk the floor over you
You can walk on grass, walk on sod
Walk on water if you think you're God
Walk on by, forget my name
But you can't walk back the way you came

    You can't walk back the way you came
    You can't walk back the way you came
    Walk on by, forget my name
    But you can't walk back the way you came

Hands of Time

I Come Down from My Hometown

I come down from my hometown back when I was young
Thought the world was waiting there wanting to be won
Watches needed winding then and sometimes to be set
Women were for finding then and most times to forget

    I walked the line for quite some time and thought I'd done enough
    Said nothing here can hurt you boy, you're too young and tough
    It's been half a century since those words were said
    Many things can hurt me now and some would leave me dead

I said the things they told me to, learned the social graces
Did the things I'm supposed to do, ran the human races
I ran fast and I ran far for mostly second places
I found and lost so many friends I can't recall their faces

    I walked the line for quite some time and thought I'd done enough
    Said nothing here can hurt you boy, you're too young and tough
    It's been half a century since those words were said
    Many things can hurt me now and some would leave me dead

Money is a jester now, the same for fame and power
They're blowing in the evening wind like a dandelion flower
Time is what I cherish now, to share a friendly glass
To love and be loved in return and hope that it will last

    I walked the line for quite some time and thought I'd done enough
    Said nothing here can hurt you boy, you're too young and tough
    It's been half a century since those words were said
    Many things can hurt me now and some would leave me dead

I Come Down from My Hometown

Hangin' 'Round the Bars in Town

The wine it flows, the money goes, the band plays their songs
And ev'ry single word I say comes out sounding wrong
The people there seem happier than they've any right to be
Hangin' 'round the bars in town for the Friday jubilee

All hope to find that special one, is this the time or place
I'm scared inside and sad in spite of the smile on my face
Old and young, have your fun, it's all the same to me
Hangin' 'round the bars in town for the Friday jubilee

    Some are shy and some are bold, some are hot and some are cold
    Some are kind and some are mean, most are somewhere in between
    Some are shiny smooth, some are lost like me
    Hangin' 'round the bars in town for the Friday jubilee

The work week's done, at least for some, payday has arrived
I lost my soul long ago, I'm trying to survive
Take a chance, risk a dance, then trudge on home
Saturday morning wake up all alone

    Some are shy and some are bold, some are hot and some are cold
    Some are kind and some are mean, most are somewhere in between
    Some are shiny smooth, some are lost like me
    Hangin' 'round the bars in town for the Friday jubilee

Hangin' 'Round the Bars in Town

Pitcher and a Glass

I've had some good times but they never last
Just bring me a pitcher and a glass
Fill it with the only gold I've ever known
Set it down beside me so I won't be so alone

    Sittin' by myself in the center of a crowd
    Tryin' hard to laugh, talkin' extra loud

Good times and friends, they always pass
Just bring me a pitcher and a glass

Outside surrounded by so many friends
Inside as lonely as I've ever been
A night like so many and I'm fadin' fast
So tip up the pitcher and top off my glass

    I heard old heartaches all fade away
    And that tomorrow will be a brand new day

But now it's tonight and all that I ask
Is bring me a pitcher and a glass

Pitcher and a Glass

The Old Brown Bottle

I'd like to take a moment if you can spare the time
Let me tell you something about this life of mine
Oh, I had my troubles and yes, I got my friends
Not the least of either is the bottle in my hand

I was young I'd drink a dozen, now I'm old I drink a few
Usually home by ten, used to stay 'til two
Now I take a table, back then I'd often stand
But it's the same old brown bottle in my hand

    Maybe it's a Bud or maybe Miller Lite
    Never had a beer that I didn't like
    You can change the place or you can change the brand
    But it's the same old brown bottle in my hand

Now if I go to heaven it surely would be nice
To find they had a cooler of bottles there on ice
No more hangovers, hallelujah amen
Just a cold wet brown bottle in my hand

    Maybe it's a Bud or maybe Miller Lite
    Never had a beer that I didn't like
    Or if the beer in heaven is Labatt's Canadian
    It'll be the same brown bottle in my hand

    The same old brown bottle in my hand

The Old Brown Bottle

Armistice Day Storm

I sat one night in a waterfront bar
My hair now thinning and white
I said to a kid there, sit where you are
And help me pass out the night

    Buy me a drink and I'll tell you a story
    Of when I was sober and when I was young
    Some of it true and some allegory
    Part can be told but part must be sung

I reached down for my coat on the floor
And took out an old ukulel'
I strummed with a thumb all calloused and sore
And sang in my quavery wail

Well I remember a certain November
The day was eleven, the year forty-one
The sky was as gray as an old pewter pitcher
We were home bound on the Kewanee run

    When the wind begun screaming, I hoped I was dreaming
    And would wake with the lake rolling slow
    The cars on the car deck were straining the chaining
    I begun crossing myself down below

The skipper was praying while he was steering
Begging for life and forgiveness of sin
But God wasn't caring or else lost his hearing
The prayer disappeared in a shriek of the wind

The devil was laughing, his hell was a burning
I felt like a mouse in a box with a cat
With little religion and even less learning
I thought that dying'd be worth more than that

Then I picked my coat up off of the floor
And tucked in the old ukulel'
I stood and faced myself to the door
That was the end of my tale

The kid cried, don't go 'cause I wanna know
Old man, did you make it and how
I grinned and I said, of course we did
Or I wouldn't be standing here now . . . oh no

But thanks for the liquor and being my friend
And hearing an old man sing
And if some day we should meet again
You know the brand that I drink

Buy me a drink and I'll tell you a story
Of when I was sober and when I was young
Some of it true and some allegory
Part can be told but part must be sung

Part can be told but part must be sung

Ships Lost on Lake Michigan in the Armistice Day Storm

SS Novadoc

SS Anna C. Minch

SS William B. Davock

Armistice Day Storm

Rollin' Along

I don't ask for pleasure, Lord, just keep me from the pain
And I don't ask for wisdom if you'll only keep me sane
We'll be rollin' along, we'll be rollin' along

I don't ask a banquet, Lord, just a bit to eat and drink
And I don't ask to swim too fast, so long as I don't sink
We'll be rollin' along, we'll be rollin' along

    The best in life is free, we heard
    Though you may argue what they say
    We only ask a little bit to help us on our way

I don't want a mansion, just a warm dry place to sleep
And I don't ask for fame renown, just some memories I can keep
We'll be rollin' along, we'll be rollin' along

I don't need dress-up clothes, just one good set of jeans
A winter coat to keep me warm and a bath to keep me clean
We'll be rollin' along, we'll be rollin' along

    We don't ask an aged wine, just a cool beer in our hand
    And we don't ask for stocks and bonds, just a pay check now and then

I don't ask eternal life, you can give away my share
And paradise as well unless, my best friends all are there
We'll be rollin' along, we'll be rollin' along

We'll be rollin' along, we'll be rollin' along
We'll be rollin' along, we'll be rollin' along

Rollin' Along

No Fool Like an Old Fool

Once I had a home where I went when work was done
Had a loving woman, a daughter and a son
I left it all behind me when I heard the devil call
There's no fool like an old fool and I'm the biggest fool of all

The Devil, when he's working moves in mysterious ways
He has a bag of tricks that he gleefully plays
And the longer you live the further you fall
There's no fool like an old fool and I'm the biggest fool of all

Sometimes I sit in taverns and may ask someone to dance
After winking at a friend she may give me a chance
You can shout it from the mountain, you can hear the echo fall
There's no fool like an old fool and I'm the biggest fool of all

        You can write it in the paper, you can write it on the wall
        Emblazon it in letters eight or nine feet tall
        There's no fool like an old fool and I'm the biggest fool of all

No Fool Like an Old Fool

Lie of the Mind

Tell me why are some so lonely without a single friend
For others life's a party that never seems to end
Why are some so happy while others are so sad
Or made so very bitter by the fun they never had
Oh why are some so cruel and others are so kind
Why are the reasons so very hard to find
Could it all be only a lie of the mind

Why are some so cold and others are so hot
Some so very lucky and some, well, they're not
How do some walk so directly on a road that never winds
Their orders sure and certain, all notarized and signed
Some see so clearly and some are nearly blind
Why are the reasons so very hard to find
Could it all be only a lie of the mind

Why do some stay together and others drift apart
Some go on laughing and others break their heart
Why is it so common for some to grudge and hate
While others fast forget or shrug it off as fate
Why do some walk ahead and others lag behind
Why are the reasons so very hard to find
Could it all be only a lie of the mind

        A lie of the mind, a lie of the mind
        Could it all be only a lie of the mind

Lie of the Mind

To Say Goodbye

There's been so many times I've had to say goodbye
To women that I loved and friends who have died
To forests they cut down and fields they subdivide
There's been so many times I've had to say goodbye

You take the lowly jack pine, such a humble tree
They pulped it all away, turned into O S B
Blueberries beneath, left to burn and die
There's been so many times I've had to say goodbye

My dog and I once wandered where farmers planted corn
Pheasants called and nested, hatchlings there were born
Now it's all paved over, no crowing roosters fly
They slipped away in silence, left me to say goodbye

There's been so many times I've had to say goodbye
To women that I loved and friends who have died
To forests they cut down and fields they subdivide
There's been so many times I've had to say goodbye

Friends that cared about me as if I were their son
Fishing laughing singing, they filled my life with fun
But one by one I heard the tolling of the bell
There's been so many times I've had to say farewell

And as for the women, the bewilderment and pain
I'd just soon let it pass and sing the chorus again

There's been so many times we've had to say goodbye
To forests they clear cut and fields they subdivide
Let us drink a toast and raise our glasses high
To all that we love and friends who have died

To all that we love and friends who have died

To Say Goodbye

Suino's Song

The North Branch, the West Branch, branch up from the south
High Bridge to Reed and Green, down to the mouth
Steelhead in May, brook trout in June
Some stay too long, some leave too soon

    Two Hearted River, it's hard to say goodbye
    Two Hearted River, Proshchai, Proshchai

A bar stool is a barstool, just a place to sit
Grand Marais, West Liberty, it matters not a bit
But there's an empty bar stool in more than one saloon
Marks the place of one who surely left too soon

    Two Hearted River, hard to say goodbye
    Two Hearted River, Proshchai, Proshchai

A puzzle is a puzzle, just to pass the time
The answers soon forgotten like a riddle or a rhyme
But unlike the puzzle from Old Town to the Dunes
Let us not forget one who left too soon

    Two Hearted River, hard to say goodbye
    Two Hearted River, Proshchai, Proshchai

Farewell to One and All

    The time has come to say goodnight
    Farewell to one and all
    Goodbye to you my Grand Marais
    Farewell my Mackinac

Goodbye you birches gleaming white
You spruce so straight and black
Goodbye you aspen frail as life
You pine and tamarack

    The time has come to say goodnight
    Farewell to one and all
    Goodbye to you my Grand Marais
    Farewell my Mackinac

Goodbye to you my River Fox
God bless your rusty flow
May the trout who frolic there
Be pleased to see me go

    The time has come to say goodnight
    Farewell to one and all
    Goodbye to you my Grand Marais
    Farewell my Mackinac

Lake Superior Shore

Farewell to One and All

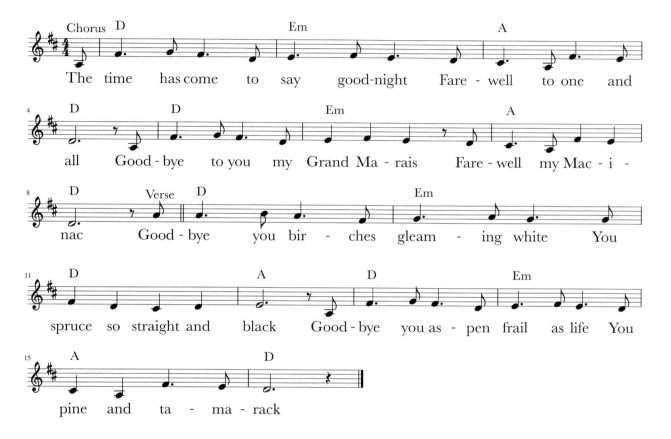

Hey Buddy, It's Still Me

Once I was a young man, I dreamed a young man's dreams
I hunted in the low land and fished the brushy streams
I courted pretty women, danced the whole night through
Thought spring would last forever, just April, May and June

I made a bit of money, had a lot of fun
Played away the nighttime, worked away the sun
I never thought of trouble though the years flew by
You add a month to spring time, it's still only July

Then my friends grew older, some even passed away
The fields they turned to golden, my hair turned to gray
Autumn was upon us, still how were we to know
Time would pass so very fast, oh lord, where did it go

Now I am an old man, I dream an old man's dreams
No longer hunt the low land or fish the brushy streams
My body's but a costume now, well weathered you can see
Still here inside this disguise, hey buddy, it's still me

Jay as the Old Man in Old Man in Love, *June 2013*

Hey Buddy, It's Still Me

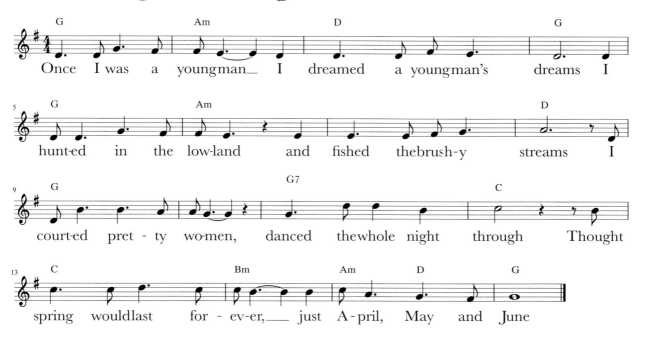

Destruction's Its Own Penalty

Jay's songs of destruction from wars and industrial greed teach us history not found in the standard textbooks. He is a teacher of "alternative" history that gives us truth. And while the stories themselves can be depressing, Jay's music can inspire change — hopefully, creating a world of peace and conscious caring for our planet's environment.

Charlie Weaver, Musician and Fisherman, Jim O'Dell in every production of the *North Country Opera* except one

Liam O'Reilly

My name is Liam O'Reilly and from Boston I am come
My father was a soldier back in World War I
The Brits took him from Galway and sent him to the Marne
My mom become a widow shortly after I was born

An aunt living in Boston invited Mom and me
We boarded ship in Dublin and sailed across the sea
I arrived at manhood when World War II began
They sent me off to Normandy to save the Brits again

From Cherbourg to the Rhine I never took a scratch
Some were not so lucky and many did not come back
When it was over there here again I came
To marry Mary O'Holleran, as Irish as her name

Soon we had a son, we called him Paddy Joe
The name, it was his grandfather's so very long ago
A score of years flew by, he too became a man
Just about the time another war began

We're not the ones to shirk, my own father nor me
The lad he had a heart at the age of twenty three
Some said the war was wicked, that it was bound to fail
Many went to Canada, some even went to jail

But Paddy went to Vietnam to fight the foreign war
And do the royal bidding as his people had before
Though I prayed in private and Mary went to Mass
The enemy in Asia had other gods, I guess

So we lost our Paddy Joe in far-off Vietnam
We remain in Boston where the nation first began
The wars go on and on, but all I know they done
They took away my father and they took away my son

Liam O'Reilly

Linebacker from Muskegon

You used to tag along with me and go most everywhere I went when you were just a kid
And I took you hunting and fishing and I took you out to the ball game and you liked most everything we did
When you were older I'd go down to the Legion Club on Saturday nights and the boys would gather round and then
They said, "You sure must be proud of that kid, Frank, he's about the best linebacker in Muskegon since we don't know when"

Then you finally graduated and went off to the university and everything was goin' great
Even at Christmas time when you come home and said, "Dad, there just ain't no hundred eighty pound linebackers in the Big Eight"
I said, "Hang in there, kid, eat a lotta meat and potatoes, you'll grow up, just wait and see"
Though I was a bit disappointed when you dropped out of engineering and took up philosophy

Then summer time came and you come home looking strange and talking weird, it made me feel so bad
You been hangin' round with those peculiar people and listenin' to some professors that I wish you never had

> Oh, your hair hung down in curls
> You loved the floppy-chested girls
> Your mom and I just prayed and wrung our hands
> The old red white and blue meant nothing more to you
> So you sewed it on the seat of your pants

Well, we kinda lost track of you then, you didn't come round much anymore and all I learned was from the gossips in the town
They said you climbed up top the post office in Norman, Oklahoma and tore the Star Spangled Banner down
And a man come round in a neat gray suit, he was from the FBI
When he said you were in jail for draft dodging, it made me just wanna die

> Then you got back in town a while ago
> Mama met you at the door
> Threw her arms around her only son
> And her tears fell on the floor

Now I know you didn't murder anybody or rob anyone and you even always paid your income tax
But I admit there was a time I'd trade a manly crime or two for the yellow stripe they painted on your back
For there were other men in other jails far across the sea, praying and crying to come home
And the jailers there weren't their friends, they were little yellow men who chilled the very marrow of your bones

And the gossips, they're still busy. They say there goes poor old Frank, his kid sure done him wrong
And they don't talk about the best linebacker in Muskegon, but about some hippy coward home from jail where he belonged

> Oh, they took away your curls and all the floppy-chested girls
> They carved a couple of furrows in your brow
> But in spite of what you done, Jesus Christ, you're still my son
> I loved you as a boy, I love you now

Linebacker from Muskegon

Leave the Bottle on the Table, Waiter

        Leave the bottle on the table, waiter, I ain't finished yet
        There's been too many places I been trying to forget
        And too many faces I wish I never met
        Leave the bottle on the table, waiter, I ain't finished yet

I was just a little boy and said the Pledge in school
And on Sunday morning we learned the Golden Rule
But a small-town boy ain't got no chance to pick between the two
They wrap him up from the start in the old Red White and Blue

I learned to love my neighbor 'till they sent me off to war
They gave me fancy weapons and they showed me what they're for
I learned to pull the trigger and I hardly even winced
And shot at lot of people I got nothin' against

        Leave the bottle on the table, waiter, I ain't finished yet
        There's been too many places I been trying to forget
        And too many faces I wish I never met
        Leave the bottle on the table, waiter, I ain't finished yet

Roam around this old town, you find me sittin' here
And what's more I may say now things you don't want to hear
We lost that war anyhow but a few things become clear
The rich folks use boys like me to keep themselves secure

        Leave the bottle on the table, waiter, I ain't finished yet
        There's been too many places I been trying to forget
        And too many faces I wish I never met
        Leave the bottle on the table, waiter, I ain't finished yet

Leave the Bottle on the Table, Waiter

Are You Comin' Are You Goin'

Sometimes on a plane or in an airport bar
Seated by a stranger, no idea who they are
I will ask a question, only trying to be nice
"Are you comin' are you goin'?" Just to break the ice

Could be a pretty woman, a tired business man
Really doesn't matter, we'll never meet again
But last week in Chicago, waiting there to fly
I could not ask the question, I have tell you why

    He was dressed in desert camo, I watched him stow his tote
    "Are you comin' are you goin'?" The words stuck in my throat

His boots were sandy colored, his jacket neat and tight
I helped him get it off as he sat down on my right
He thanked and called me "sir," so young and so polite
Why oh why was he going off to fight
Wars so far away, with no end in sight

Back in basic training when he was screaming "kill"
Did he know what he was saying, was it just another drill
Was he ready to die or be maimed at least
How much did he know about the Middle East

    Or had he been before, now going back again
    He was but a child when it all began

So I bit my tongue, there was nothing I could say
Might well ask the weather, how's it look out there today?
Is it rainin', is it snowin'
Is it still or is it blowin'
Are the rivers full and flowin'
Are they shrinkin', are they growin'
Are you doubtin', are you knowin'
Are you reapin', are you sowin'
But never, ever, ever . . .
. . . are you comin' are you goin'

Are You Comin' Are You Goin'

Turning the World into Texas

When rich people's taxes by the billions go down
And everything green is turning to brown
Then you may ask as you look around
Are they turning the world into Texas

When freedom of religion means Christian, that's it
By slim chance a Jew if he hedges a bit
When the Great Lakes are drained and the profits they made
Are invested off shore, and no taxes are paid
Then you will know, too late I'm afraid
They're turning the world into Texas

    Turning the world into Texas
    Turning the world into Texas
    Then you will know, too late I'm afraid
    They're turning the world into Texas

When all of our songbooks are right-Christian hymnals
And all of our leaders are white-collar criminals
All of our forests are derricks and trash
And all of our news is bought with their cash
Then you will know, you won't have to ask
They're turning the world into Texas

    Turning the world into Texas
    Turning the world into Texas
    Then you will know, you won't have to ask
    They're turning the world into Texas

When things go wrong, they just start a war
Break out the flag, call an encore
Dress all their ladies in red white and blue
Kiss all the babies and rich oil men too
Then you will know what you already knew
They're turning the world into Texas

This last verse may offend some people here
So cover your children's tender young ears
They can dress all their ladies in red white and blue
Kiss all the babies and my ass too
But up here there'll always be more than a few
Who won't let them do what they want to do
Turn the whole world into Texas

CENTRAL CREEK MINE TAILINGS, KEWEENAW COUNTY, MI

Turning the World into Texas

Never Been to Dixie

I never been to Dixie, don't sound like much to me
Drinking too-sweet whiskey, eatin' black-eyed peas
The winters are so warm they say you can't tell when it's spring
I've never been to Dixie, don't think I missed a thing

I never seen the Suwanee or Tallahatchie Bridge
Don't know the Shenandoah or the old Blue Ridge
My heart is in the northland with the winter ice and snow
I've never been to Dixie, and I don't plan to go

>   Never been to Dixie, all I know's what I been told
>   The snakes all carry poison, and there's trash along the road

But I do like Jimmy Rogers and the old songs of the south
You can tell it by the tune now slippin' from my mouth
And I will admit affection for the fiddle of Bob Wills
Though I never been to Texas and I hope I never will

Never seen a Georgia moon or Kentucky, Tennessee's
The moon that shines on Michigan looks good enough for me
From Maine to Minnesota it's not hard to know
Why I never been to Dixie and I don't plan to go

>   **Spoken:**
>   (*Well folks, not long ago I had to pass through a part of Dixie,
>   so I had to write a little coda to this song.*)

I finally got to Dixie, there I learned some things
How they love Rush Limbaugh, though some think he's too left-wing
And oh they hate the Clintons, though Bill is one of them
For Arkansas's as Dixie as any place I been

They hate the United Nations, why I just can't say
Seems it's done very little in the southern USA
They love assault weapons, and quite a few are bought
And oh how they love Jesus, but not the things he taught

>   I finally got to Dixie, it's worse than what I thought

Never Been to Dixie

Tittabawassee Jane

      Tittabawassee Jane's her name, Tittabawassee Jane
      The river there must be named after her
      She's Tittabawassee Jane

I met her in Midland Michigan a long long time ago
She loved me down on the edge of town
Where the Tittabwassee flows

      Tittabawassee Jane's her name, Tittabawassee Jane
      The river there must be named after her
      She's Tittabawassee Jane

She worked at the old Dow Chemical plant
I waited for her shift to end
She made napalm or some kind of bomb
But I wasn't too political then

The air it smelled like kerosene
Whatever Dow blew out
The river was laced with lumps of waste
Called Tittabawassee trout

      Tittabawassee Jane's her name, Tittabawassee Jane
      The river there must be named after her
      She's Tittabawassee Jane

I haven't been back in quite some time
But the company magazine
Says the air blows fresh in Midland Mich
And the Tittabawassee's clean

Now I won't tell you what to believe
Dow's been known to lie
Though we all care what they do to the air
The Tittabawassee's mine

      Tittabawassee Jane's her name, Tittabawassee Jane
      The river there must be named after her
      She's Tittabawassee Jane (yodel)

Tittabawassee Jane

The Tittabawassee River Near the Dow Chemical Plant in Midland, MI

Where Have All the White Pines Gone, Daddy

Where have all the white pines gone, Daddy
That grew so long ago
Gone for the houses of Colonel McCormick's friends
In the city of Chicago

Where have all the dune beaches gone, Daddy
That burned our feet so hot
To high-rise chalets with wrought iron porches
And private marinas for yachts

Where have all the morels gone, Daddy
That you hunted on your knees
Buried alive 'neath I-75
So the Fords can go north with ease

Where have all the meadows gone, Daddy
Where the pheasant used to run
Gone for profit and to line the pocket
Of rich men every one

    Where have all the brook trout gone, Daddy
    That set your heart in a spin
    Poisoned with silt from the bridges they built
    For the folks at the Holiday Inn

Where will it all end, Daddy
Will any be left for me
I don't know, my son, if the worst's been done
But destruction's its own penalty

        I don't know, my son, if the worst's been done
        But destruction's its own penalty

Where Have All the White Pines Gone, Daddy

Where have all the white pines gone, Daddy / That grew so long ago / Gone for the houses of Colonel McCormick's friends / In the city of Chicago / Where have all the brook trout gone, Daddy / That set your heart in a spin / Poisoned with silt from the bridges they built / For the folks at the Holiday Inn

Clear-cut White Pine Plain, Alger County, MI

Same Folks We Hated in High School

It's the same folks we hated in high school
That are still leaning on us today
It's the same folks we hated in high school
They trump ev'ry high card we play

The man in the bank who said he didn't think
He could let me have a loan I really need
Was the class president, the faculty pet
And most likely to succeed

The woman who rules by the country club pool
Always so tan and so lean
Was a drum majorette and I'm willing to bet
A virgin homecoming queen

And the man with the star who searched my whole car
To tell me one taillight was out
Was the male secretary in the school library
And the town's first Eagle Scout

    It's the same folks we hated in high school
    That are still leaning on us today
    It's the same folks we hated in high school
    They trump every high card we play

The quarterback now is a rich obstetrician
He positions his hands much the same
Though his body has softened and he fumbles less often
The fees are worth more than the fame

And the girl who squealed to the teacher in charge
When we snuck the beer in the dance
Was on a jury last week that convicted a freak
Of growing unusual plants

    It's the same folks we hated in high school
    That are still leaning on us today
    It's the same folks we hated in high school
    They trump every high card we play

Same Folks We Hated in High School

Score Transcription Credits

Transcribed by Edie Herrold:
Black River Jones; Farewell to One and All; A Fool for Lovin' You; Hangin' 'Round the Bars in Town; Hey Buddy, It's Still Me; I Come Down from My Hometown; Liam O'Reilly; Lie of the Mind; Never Been to Dixie; Pitcher and a Glass; Rollin' Along; Same Folks We Hated in High School; Suino's Song; The Old Brown Bottle; Times That We Had; Where Have All the White Pines Gone, Daddy

Transcribed by David Roof:
Are You Comin' Are You Goin'; Cross Over the Line; Hands Of Time; I Love Two Rivers and Only One Woman; I'm Singing; It's a Wonder; Leave the Bottle on the Table, Waiter; Manistee Waltz; The Lake; Tittabawassee Jane

Transcribed by Nikola L. Whallon:
Armistice Day Storm; Baker's Daughter; Barbara's Waltz; Boats Came into Ludington; Cut River Bridge; Darlin' Except You; Don't Let Me Down Easy; Far Side of the Bed; Fragile Thing; Going Home; Heaven for Me; I'll Remember; Last Night You Came Alive Again; Linebacker from Muskegon; Lord, What Do We Know; Most I'm Missing You; Never Been Much of a Ramblin' Man; No Fool Like an Old Fool; November Love; Read Between the Lines; Red Rose; Road Less Traveled; So Easy; To Say Goodbye; Turning the World into Texas; Wednesday's Child

Illustration Credits

frontispiece Photo by Jeffrey R. Parsons
p. vii Photo by Nada Rakic
p. xv Photo by Michael Smith, 2014 production *Old Man in Love*, Trinity House Theater, Livonia, MI
p. xvi Photo courtesy of Jay Stielstra
p. xvii Photo courtest of Jay Stielstra
p. xviii Mr. Flood's Party calendar created by CrowQuill Graphics, April 1977, Photo by Barbara Schmid
p. xix Photo by Barbara Schmid
p. xxi Photo by Suzanne Dooley-Hash, courtesy of Barbara Schmid
pp. 1, 15, 18, 19, 33, 34, 40, 41, 45, 49, 64, 80, 96, 105, 113 Artwork by Kay Clahassey
p. 4 Painting by Jim Lounsbury, picture courtesy of Barbara Schmid
p. 6 Photo by Barbara Schmid
p. 9 Photo by Nada Rakic
p. 10 Photo by Nada Rakic
p. 13 Photo by Nada Rakic
p. 16 Photo by Nada Rakic

(Illustration Credits continued)

p. 22 Photo by Nada Rakic
p. 23 Photo by Barbara Schmid
p. 24 Photo by Craig Jaffe
p. 28 Photo by Nada Rakic
p. 31 Photo by Barbara Schmid
p. 37 Photo courtesy of Robert Whallon
p. 47 Photo by Nada Rakic
p. 52 Photo by Craig Jaffe
p. 54 Photo by Kay Clahassey
p. 56 Drawing by Nada Rakic
p. 60 Photo by Kay Clahassey
p. 66 Photo by Kay Clahassey
p. 70 Photo by Barbara Schmid
p. 73 Photo courtesy of Barbara Schmid
p. 74 Photo by Nada Rakic
p. 78 Photo by Kay Clahassey
p. 86 Photos reproduced by permission of the Center for Archival Collections, Jerome Library, Bowling Green State University
p. 98 Photo by Barbara Schmid
p. 100 Photo courtesy of Barbara Schmid
p. 103 Photo reproduced by permission of the Interfaith Council for Peace and Justice, Ann Arbor, MI
p. 117 Photo by Dennis Albert
p. 123 Drawing by Jamie Valen, courtesy of Barbara Schmid
p. 125 Photo by Dennis Albert

Jay Stielstra Discography

Times That We Had – 2002, recorded with Jay's band The Country Quartet (Jay Stielstra, Gary Munce, Kelly Schmidt, Paul Winder)

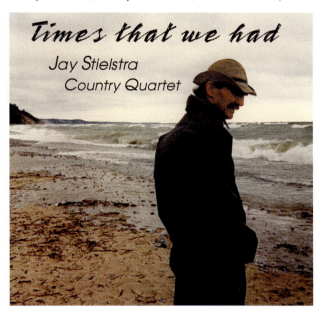

Cross Over the Line
Manistee River Waltz
It's a Wonder
Road Less Traveled
Red Rose
No Fool Like an Old Fool
I'm Singin'
I Love Two Rivers and Only One Woman
Hey Buddy, It's Still Me
A Fool For Lovin' You
Times that We Had
Going Home

Don't Let Me Down Easy – 2009, recorded with the Jay Stielstra Trio (Jay Stielstra, Judy Banker, John Sayler)

Don't Let Me Down Easy
November Love
Tittabawassee Jane
Manistee River Waltz
There Was a Time
The Lake
Leave the Bottle on the Table, Waiter
I'll Remember
Same Folks We Hated in High School
Last Night You Came Alive Again
It's a Wonder

Michigan In Song – 2013, compilation disc of Jay's songs about Michigan performed by Jay and by other well-known Michigan artists

Cross Over the Line (Jay Stielstra and the Country Quartet)
I'm Singin' (Mustard's Retreat)
I Love Two Rivers and Only One Woman (Michael Smith with the North Country Opera Band)
Never Been Much of a Ramblin' Man (David Menefee with the North Country Opera Band)
Heaven for Me (Charlie Weaver with the North Country Opera Band)
The Lake (Jay Stielstra Trio)
Tittabawassee Jane (Chris Buhalis)
Boats Came in to Ludington (Charlie Weaver with the North Country Opera Band)
The Manistee River Waltz (Jay Stielstra Trio)
Going Home (Chris Buhalis)

Heaven for Me – 2017, recorded with musical friends Judy Banker, Dave Roof, Jason Dennie, Peter Madcat Ruth, and Mary Seelhorst

Heaven for Me
Never Been Much of a Ramblin' Man
Wednesday's Child
Never Been to Dixie
Read Between the Lines
Pitcher and a Glass
La Gran Allegria
Turning the World into Texas
Most I'm Missing You
So Easy
Baker's Daughter
Are You Comin' Are You Goin'

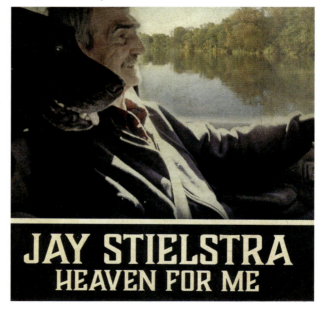

To request a CD, send an email with the title you are requesting, your name and mailing address to: jaystielstrasongs@gmail.com
For other information: facebook.com/jaystielstratrio